Copyright © 2015 by Mike Mongo
All rights reserved.
Written by Mike Mongo.
Edited by Kim Keller.
Design by MacFadden & Thorpe.
Published by Inkshares, Inc., San Francisco, California
Printed in China.

First Edition
1 2 3 4 5 6 7 8 9 10
Library of Congress Control Number: 2015938853
ISBN 978-1-941758-16-8
(paperback)

THE ASTRONAUT INSTRUCTION MANUAL

INKSHARES

SAN FRANCISCO

THE ASTRONAUT INSTRUCTION MANUAL

PRACTICAL SKILLS FOR FUTURE SPACE EXPLORERS

MIKE MONGO

*"In order to stay on Earth,
we are going to have to
learn how to leave it."*

—Mike Mongo

Contents

Foreword by future astronaut and Mars walker Alyssa Carson

I've wanted to be an astronaut for as long as I can remember. I learned what an astronaut was when I was three, watching Nick Jr. There they were: space explorers.

I asked my dad, "Are you an astronaut?"
"No," he said.
Then I asked him, "Can I be an astronaut?"
"Yes," he said.

Some of us love NASCAR, while others obsess over Taylor Swift. My love and obsession is space. As I grew up, I realized I didn't just want to go to space—I didn't just want to leave Earth. I wanted to go somewhere. I wanted to go to Mars.

The problem was that nobody around me was interested in space or knew anything about how to become an astronaut. I didn't have a space teacher and couldn't find a guide to becoming an astronaut. I started by reading and learning everything I could about space and the history of space exploration. And when I was seven, my father and I went on a parent-child trip to space camp in Huntsville, Alabama. It was the best weekend of my life, and I fell even more in love with space.

Four years ago, at the Sally Ride Science Festival, I was lucky enough to sit down and chat with Sandra Magnus. Sandra is an amazing astronaut. She once spent 134 days in orbit, and she was on the final mission of the Space Shuttle. I asked her when she decided to be an astronaut. She quickly told me, "When I was nine."

What I learned from Sandra was that being an astronaut isn't just a job you get as an adult; it's a dream you chase from an early age.

This book, *The Astronaut Instruction Manual,* is an awesome guide and a great first step toward each of our futures in space. It's got cool tips, introduces important people and facts, and—most importantly—helps you think like an astronaut.

We are tomorrow's astronauts. We aren't just leaving Earth. We're going somewhere—beginning with Mars, and moving onward to the distant reaches of space.

We are the Mars Generation.

**Alyssa Carson,
call sign "Blueberry"**

Alyssa Carson, 13, has ambitions of one day walking on Mars, a dream she's held since age three. In pursuit of this goal, she has attended space camps across the world, from Huntsville, Alabama, to Izmir, Turkey. Alyssa writes and speaks frequently on the matter of manned missions to Mars, including delivering a recent TEDx Talk on this subject in Kalamata, Greece.

Hello.

My name is Mike Mongo, and I am an astronaut teacher. Students call me Mr. Mike or Mr. Mongo, and I am here to train you to be ready to go to space.

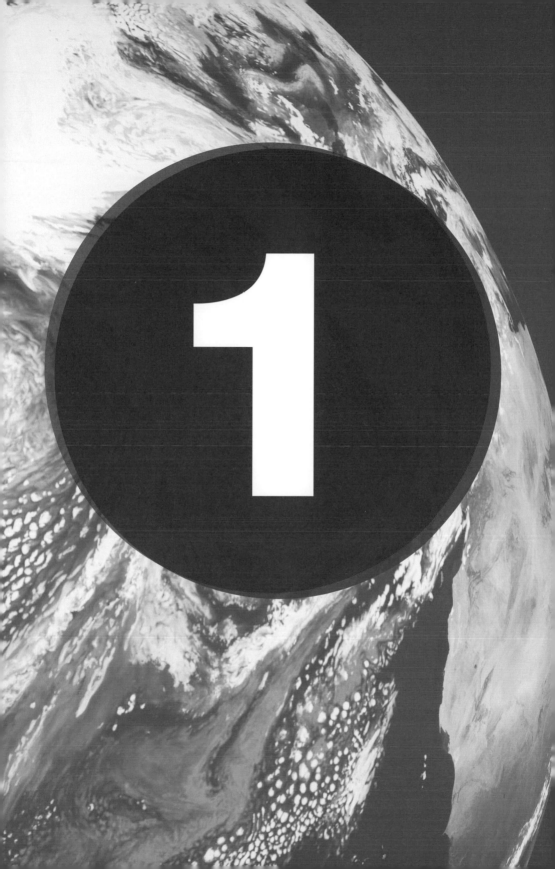

 Humannaire

If you are thinking of a career in space, in order for you to get to space, you must believe one important thing: By the time I am a young adult, I can start to live, work, and play in space as one of the next kind of astronaut, a **HUMANNAIRE.***

And that is the single most important thing for you to believe to be able to leave the planet and *live in space!*

*Note:

"Humannaire" rhymes with "human rare."

In fact, write it out below now, sign it, and date it.

"I am going to live in space. I am a HUMANNAIRE!"

"
_____

_____

_____!"

signature: _____

date: _____

If you are not yet in high school, the next few years are going to be the most important for you if you plan on being one of the next kind of astronaut, a **HUMANNAIRE**, by the time you are in your 20s.

You are going to have to study with dedication the school subjects you love best, and be well-studied even on subjects you love less. You are going to have to befriend others like yourself, others who are dedicated to going to space. And most important, you are going to have to get your own mind ready for space, because **YOU** are going to live in outer space.

Like many of us, you are planning on becoming a space-dwelling human being.

That makes you a **HUMANNAIRE!**

BY THE WAY, WHAT ARE YOUR THREE FAVORITE SUBJECTS?

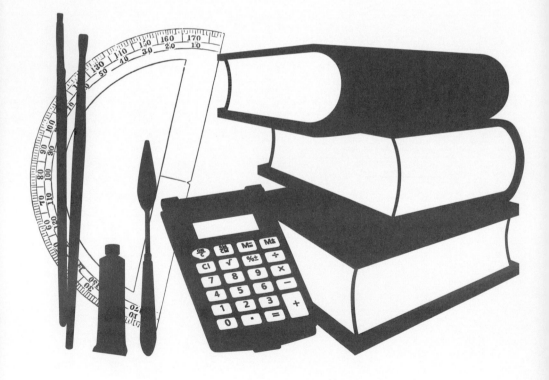

1. _____

2. _____

3. _____

It is important to let your family and closest friends know that your plans are to be a **HUMANNAIRE** and to live off-planet, so as to build support for your dream.

You will learn quickly who supports you in your quest to be a member of the first generation of deep space travelers from Planet Earth.

You see, astronauts (and cosmonauts and spationauts and taikonauts and gaganauts) are people from Earth who visit space to do work and research, but we **HUMANNAIRES** are people who will actually leave Earth... *to live in space.*

You are one of the first generation of "spacers," "off-worlders," and "space-hoppers," one of *the* **HUMANNAIRES** *from Planet Earth.* It means you are one of the people who will actually leave *Earth... to live in space!*

Can you get signatures of at least two other people who support your decision to go to space and become a HUMANNAIRE?

1. _____

2. _____

3. _____

Space will be very dangerous. You will confront grave perils, and your survival will depend on your preparedness and focus.

But before then, people like me are going to do everything in our power to ensure that you, young **HUMANNAIRE**, have the proper tools to successfully overcome any number of extraordinary circumstances.

How we are going to do this is to make sure you are emotionally equipped to face up to any given challenge.

In other words, to make you ready for living in space, we are going to use tools of the mind.

Ⓑ Tools of the Mind

Tools of the mind are the best kinds of tools. Tools of the mind are tools we already have but must discover and learn to use. One of these tools is practicing your power to slow time.

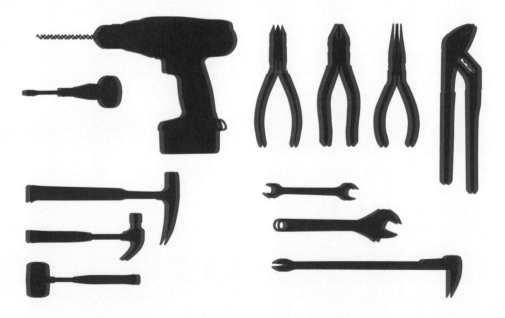

Look at a clock.* Watch the seconds pass. Watch closely. Get in rhythm with the passing seconds. Count with the seconds passing. One. One. One. One. One. One. One… keep going. Just keep going.

Now pay attention to what is happening around you between each second:

- **WHAT SOUNDS DO YOU HEAR?**
- **HOW MUCH SOUND HAPPENS IN ONE SECOND?**
- **AND THE NEXT?**
- **AND THE NEXT?**
- **KEEP IT UP.**
- **WHILE WATCHING THE CLOCK, NOTICE EVERYTHING THAT IS HAPPENING EACH SECOND.**

*Here's a useful tip:

Most smartphones have stopwatches. It is usually an app called "Clock." You can use a phone's Clock app to practice this tool of the mind and to slow time.

Another second. Where are you? Another second. How do you feel? Another second. Where are you now? Another second. How do you feel now?

Suddenly, without you actually realizing it, time slows down around you almost to a near stop.

See how it works yet? Just keep practicing. We all have the power to slow time. That is a mighty power.

Interestingly, it is a power we forget we have. That is why we must practice practicing.

Practice practicing is what people mean by FOCUS.

There is a tremendous advantage to learning the power of focus. Living is dangerous: just as people die on Earth, people will die in space.

To live and to *not* die in space, we must be prepared and focused. This is why the very first tool of the mind for successfully living in space is focus.

The secret to living a good life in space is appreciating how life is so much like a very fun game. How genuinely focused you play determines how successful a life you will have.

© Extraordinary People

A well-played game of life can be something genuinely extraordinary.

STEVE "THE CROCODILE HUNTER" IRWIN

The life of wildlife expert Steve "The Crocodile Hunter" Irwin is an excellent example of how this is true. He did what he loved doing best all the way to the end—and he died doing what he loved. Steve Irwin died in the line of duty, and he was focused.

FELIX BAUMGARTNER

Another good example is daredevil and sky jumper Felix Baumgartner. He learned focus so well, he became the first person to jump to Earth from the edge of space and break through the sound barrier doing so.

SHELLY-ANN FRASER-PRYCE

With focus, runner Shelly-Ann Fraser-Pryce won Olympic gold medals. It was also focus that kept her eye on the prize while growing up from humble beginnings in Jamaica. Her focus is leading her on toward becoming the fastest woman in the world.

ALAN EUSTACE

And now Alan Eustace, a computer scientist who works at Google, has broken Felix Baumgartner's record! Alan Eustace is a great example of focus. For three years, he and others worked on the design of his spacesuit—it was like a spaceship suit—and he had to be super disciplined and focused during his jump from space.*

On this we can all agree: it is better to do what you love and to live out your dreams than not to do what you love and go through life without having lived out your dreams.

*Note:

Incidentally, what is Alan Eustace's new world record? Google *Alan Eustace jump world record*.

Simple, right? Yet what many non-astronauts and non-**HUMANNAIRES** fail to see is how doing what you love makes it fun to be focused. In other words, doing what you love makes life extraordinary, but what makes doing what you love so extraordinary is focus.

The key is FOCUS.

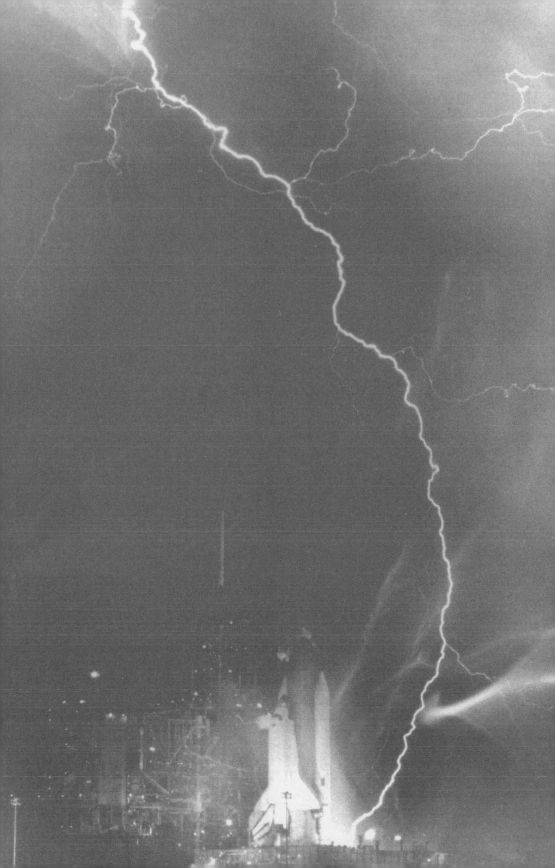

Ⓓ What Will Life Be Like?

Our life's end does not have to be the end of us, but it is the end of our turn. So when and if we have to die, make the end of your turn be the completion of an extraordinary life story.

Yet if you can, why not just keep on living? If you can successfully avoid getting hit by a runaway train, or having a helicopter drop out of the sky on you, or any other unluckiness which today might lead to your demise, and do so at least until the time that you are 20 years of age, chances are you will live another 100 years... or more!

Such is the promise of humankind's technological direction at the very beginning of the 21st century. Exactly how you will live another 100 years after age 20, or what happens to make it so, will be a surprise. It wouldn't be called a surprise if we knew precisely what amazing things were to happen or exactly how such things were going to take place!

There is no telling what discoveries and advancements will be made over the coming years!

Consider this.

In the first decade of the 20th century, society was without telephones, automobiles, lightbulbs, airplanes, or even radios almost anywhere.

Most of the world had not even heard of electricity—because at that time, it took scientists and researchers nearly three months' time to communicate new ideas and discoveries to the rest of the world.

Nonetheless, by 1920—only 10 years later—telephones, radios, lightbulbs, airplanes, and automobiles were seen all over the world!

And at that time, the whole world worked together to build highways and runways and skyscrapers, and to put up electric power poles and radio towers—as fast as possible!

In just nine years, our world changed from "horse driven" to "automobile driven," and everyone alive then helped make it happen together.

Now think about this.

Back around 1915, it took three entire months to send mail from one place to another. And then another three months to get a reply!

But by 1924, everyone alive discovered and experienced a world that had been completely reinvented.

Jump forward again 100 years to the present, the beginning of the 21st century. We have even more discoveries and more inventions.

We have antibiotics, X-rays, microwaves, jet planes, nuclear submarines, and space vehicles that have taken humankind to the moon and further!

We have satellites, fiber optics, silicon chips, video games, personal computers—plus all sorts of other inventions, discoveries, devices, utilities, and tools, some of which are still unfolding, like the Internet.

Where 100 years ago it took three months to get a letter from one place to another, with the Internet, it now takes just three seconds to transmit mail to anywhere on the planet. Distance hardly makes a difference. Just as our predecessors' horse-drawn buggies were replaced by automobiles and airplanes, today there are space elevators, antimatter, invisibility, and quantum transportation. For **HUMANNAIRES**, space travel will become the new reality.

It is important for you to understand that **HUMANNAIRES**—that is, people dreaming of going up to explore space and live off-planet—have always been around. **HUMANNAIRES** are the people who dreamed of flying and who desired to explore new territories.

Trailblazing is our nature. Yet for the first time, dreams of exploring and of flying and living in space have become reality. So while you dream of traveling the stars, be sure to remember those who came before us—who lived their lives and took their turns to the best of their abilities, given the resources available to them at the time—and realize we are part of a long and illustrious heritage.

We are **HUMANNAIRES** from Planet Earth!

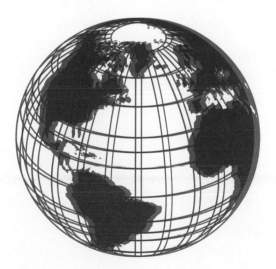

Astronauts, cosmonauts, spationauts, taikonauts, gaganauts...

...paved the way for us. 'Nauts were actually the first trailblazers to get off Planet Earth and out into space.

In their time, and even still today, 'nauts were unlike any other humans alive. **'NAIRES** are unlike even 'nauts. We are the first humans not just to get out, but to move out—to space!

HUMANNAIRES may be a new type of humankind: *space*-humans.

Some Earth-humans alive today are going to be space-humans from Planet Earth and make the permanent transition from Planet Earth to space as **HUMANNAIRES.***

Remember: every one of us **HUMANNAIRES** are *trailblazers*, blazing the pathways for others to follow and use behind us. (And for us to use again!)

Another reality to consider is the possibility of star travel—actual travel from our star system to another star system—that takes us outside of the ordinary time stream.

Only fellow star travelers will age at the same pace as us. People living on Earth, and even those living in space here in our solar system, will age years in what passes as days or minutes for us...

...that is, until we figure out a way around the speed of light.

*Question:

But why not just *visit* space and come back to Earth?

Naturally, many will. And for many, this will be good enough. But in order to live in space, real adjustments should be made that must be kept under consideration.

One is that real space travel definitely changes us physiologically.*

And in order to really be **HUMANNAIRES**—Earth humans living in space—we may be unable to freely go back and forth from Earth to space due to these changes (whether the changes are from living in space or from medical and physiological "tweaks" that *will* have to be made).

In fact, so great is the magnitude of the effects of moving to space, many will think of us **HUMANNAIRES** as people who are making great sacrifices for the betterment of all.

*Task:

Google *physiological.*
Google *Io.*

And while our space exploration will be filled with dangers and perils, and while our actions will produce many rewards and advancements for all, in the end, space exploration is our evolutionary destiny.

Space exploration is who we are. At last! As human beings untethered from gravity, unbound we will move freely throughout space and become who we are meant to be. Move to the moon or Mars! Set up shop somewhere in the asteroid belt or on Io,* the moon of Jupiter!

Or never touch ground again and live on a space station, in a space city—or even solve how to be able to live in space *as if it were just like living underwater*.

Imagine: Living in space like a fish lives freely in water, able to travel through space and the cosmos without a spacesuit at all!

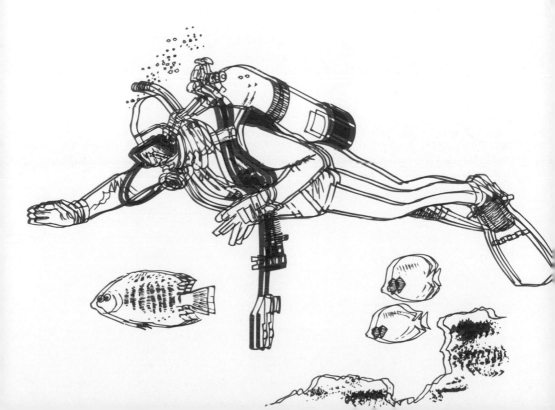

I mentioned how space travel will change our makeup, both *physiologically* and *chronologically*.* Study these changes and become familiar with the challenges to be encountered living in space.

The single greatest resource each of us has is our mind. Being able to think on the go is important. Micro seconds will count. Often there will be no second chance.

Until we have personal force fields protecting us from harm, until we can live without breathing or exposed to the vacuum of space or without having to drink water or eat food, until we are immune to the very nature of space itself, space will not be our friend.

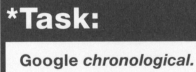

*Task:

Google *chronological*.

This is Christa McAuliffe. She was a schoolteacher and was one of seven crew members killed when the Space Shuttle *Challenger* exploded 73 seconds after launch in 1986 (pictured on next page). The explosion of *Challenger* is the greatest tragedy in NASA's history and a reminder of the ever-present danger that exists not only out there in space but even in getting up there.

(A) Getting Prepared

Space will be unpredictable and dangerous and unforgiving—as the sea has been to sailors, the desert has been to travelers, the cold to explorers.

Therefore, be ready to: grasp the situation, react, save your life, and your pals! In space, we always have to be ready to **GRASP** so that our next breath isn't our last "gasp"!

Grasp.
ReAct.
Save.
Pals.

That's **GRASP!**

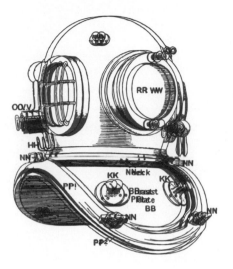

CHAPTER 2

Speaking of "gasp," here is another trick to practice focus. It is a good one. It is learning to hold your breath.

Like the trick to slow down time, you can use a clock or stopwatch. Except when it comes to holding your breath, the trick is to let time pass without noticing it. The focus is on everything but time.

When you first practice holding your breath, it may be for only a short time, even 10 seconds. But when you try again, do not be surprised if the next time you go to 15 seconds. Then 20 seconds.

Before you know it, you will be at 30 seconds. Then a full minute, 60 seconds. The trick is to keep track of time without noticing time.

And the trick to doing that is you must notice everything else *besides* time. Notice the sounds around you. Notice the world around you. Notice what you think about.

Notice your body, your arms, your brain, your feet, and, of course, your heart. Your heart will want almost as much notice as your lungs.

Then when you can wait no longer, *exhale*. But wait! Don't breathe in just yet! You see, as soon as you exhale, your body relaxes all over again. When you exhale, you have extra time—it's a great way to make a single breath last longer.

It's a trick inside of a trick.

When we are in space or underwater or in a smelly room, if you have the presence of mind to be able to hold your breath* when it is most important, then you will have given yourself a special power that may one day make the difference between life and death.

When we hold our breath, in the beginning, our body wants to breathe. Practicing holding your breath is like teaching your body to trust your head to run the show.

This is why keeping "your head on" even in emergencies—*especially* in emergencies—is of utmost importance.

All our health, safety, and well-being may depend on one person's quick thinking and good judgment. That person may be you! But any person whose mind is in poor working order becomes a threat to themselves and possibly to all of us who may depend on them.

*Task:

*Google *hold your breath in space.* You will be surprised!

The key here is *good working order.*

Human minds all work somewhat differently from one another—never confuse differentness from unwellness or vice versa.

Trust that everything real always works out, and your mind will be unable to fail you unless you fail it.

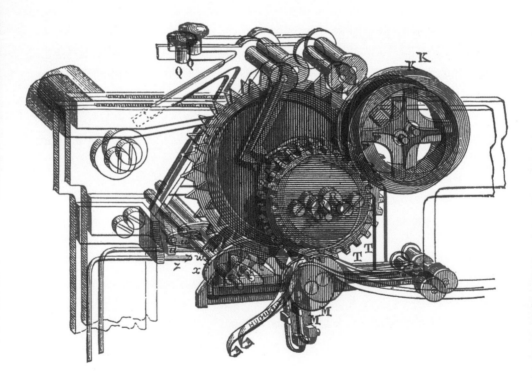

(B) Being Resource-*full*

You can fail your own mind by deluding it, misguiding it, or confusing it. But *keep* in mind, even when we are confused, if we have been honest with ourselves and to our surroundings, our minds will *always* come through for us and will never fail us.

Case in point: do you merely believe you have enough fuel, air, and water... or are you certain you do, in fact, actually have enough? There is a difference, and that difference is real. Have you had enough rest... or are you only saying you have?

Again, the difference is significant, and the more mature and experienced you get, the more significant (and noticeable) the difference will be. Being honest is one of the most simple and straightforward ways to maintain good mental hygiene.

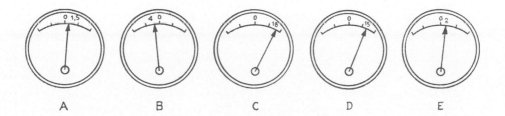

A   B   C   D   E

Even in the face of lies, the truth will always makes us happy. In fact, a great truth about truth is that "the truth makes us laugh."

That's a time-proven test for distinguishing between what is true and what is not. Facts are facts, but what is true makes you smile every time. For instance, "everything always works out."

Consider how serious some people will become who absolutely believe the opposite—that is, that everything *doesn't* work out. It's funny enough to realize, if it were true, it would make them happy.

Whenever you experience a moment, time, or period of confusion or frustration, remember to remember: "everything always works out."

It will immediately calm you down.

Then you will make decisions for action (or inaction) with a clear state of mind. When our minds are clear, everything else falls into place. Aside from our minds, our next most important valuable resource will be *whatever is around us:* equipment, tools, materials, supplies, a piece of wire, a screw, string, *whatever.*

If you knew how often a piece of metal wire—even a tiny piece of wire paper clip—has saved the day and even people's lives, *you would probably keep a paper clip on your person at all times...* just to be sure you have that piece of metal wire.

There is a saying, "one person's *refuse* is another person's *rescue*," and it applies here. What people throw away in everyday life on Earth will in space become so valuable to us that it will mean the difference between death and life.

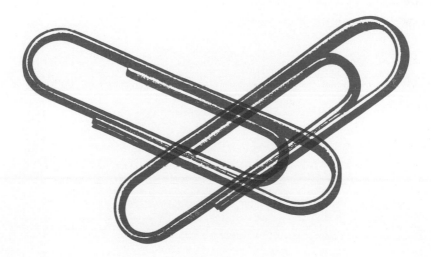

Aha! This is not to say "be a pack rat." Rather, it *is* to say "keep a smart pack." Keeping a smart pack means storing and using what you have economically and creatively and intelligently.

Do you want to learn how to be good at keeping a smart pack and, at the same time what it's like to be a space-human?

Move into a tree house. Go camping for a month. Try living aboard a sailboat or in a cave. These are experiences within reach of nearly everyone.

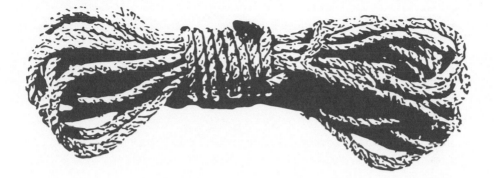

What's more, such experiments will gain you much-needed experience in making do with what you have at hand, such as the value of an empty can, a stub of a pencil, a half sheet of paper, or a broken piece of tool. Or a good string, or a section of line or rope, or a particular piece of wood. Even one single cotton swab. *Whatever!* Space-humans cannot afford to be casual about being wasteful.

HUMANNAIRES must be wise and resource-*full*. And then, in apparent contradiction to being "resource-*full*," a **HUMANNAIRE** must know when to *let something go*.

Not everything has a value, and any item's value is never greater than what it is worth to *you*.

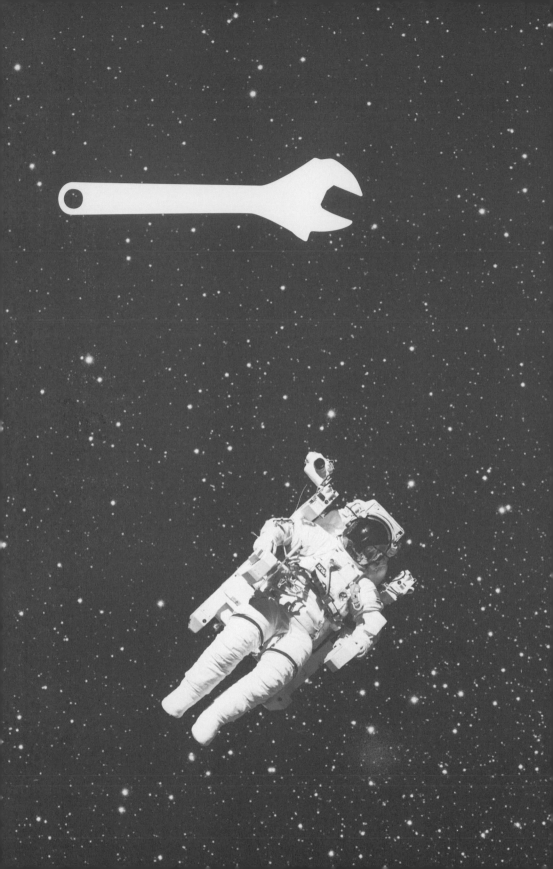

Imagine: You lose a tool or object while out in space, something that is somewhat important, but it is something that you use rarely (if ever) and that you can live without.

What if retrieving it uses up more resources than what it's worth (in fuel, air, time, etc.)? Or if you can very easily replace it? That's when it's best to let it go.

However, what if you know you can trade that tool or object that is of little value to you to *another* **HUMANNAIRE** for something that would be of terrific value to you? Then that thing would likely be worth retrieving.

And this is precisely what thinking "on the go" entails. When you are making snap judgments that have real death-or-life consequences, the absolute necessity of keeping a healthy mind and a clear head becomes obvious.

Ⓒ Strength, Flexibility & Nutrition

Physically speaking, anyone will be able to go to space. To be a **HUMANNAIRE**, you will not need legs, arms, ears, or eyes to go to space. If you do have legs, use them. If you do have arms, use them. If you can run, *run!* If you can climb, *climb!*

Strength, flexibility, and nutrition are an astronaut's best friends.

Yet physical strength, physical flexibility, and physical nutrition are only as important as the condition of our mental strength, our mental flexibility, and our mental nutrition.

Keep in mind, "garbage in, garbage out." This is true for physical health, and it is no less true for mental health. "You are what you eat" is a popular saying.

Considering how we rely on our minds to survive and succeed, wouldn't you imagine "you are what you *think*" is just as true, if not even more so?

Finally, after good mental hygiene and keeping a smart pack, the next most valuable resource a **HUMANNAIRE** has is reflex.

Reflex is action that comes without thought. Like running. Like climbing. Like breathing. Reflex is the direct result of training and repeating training (or "repetition").

You can imagine how you *may* respond in any given situation, but only the experienced among us *know* how they *do* respond. For this reason, experience must be your new best friend.

Are you afraid of heights? You won't know until you get there, so... go climb a mountain. A real mountain. Or look over a cliff.

Does motion or height or large space make you nauseous? Not sure?
Try riding a roller coaster ten times in a row. Can you eat upside down? Try it.

I won't waste my time or yours by reminding you: Be careful. Think ahead. Make plans before acting. If anything, space-humans *always* take extra caution.

Try running down a mountain path or through a forest trail, while visualizing your next step—or *your next five steps*—before you even take them. Next, do it for 20 minutes.

Now do it again. And do it again. That's repetitive experience. Repeated experience leads to real expertise.

You say you don't have mountains (or cliffs or roller coasters or forests or tall buildings) where you live? So what are you going to do?

Remember, **HUMANNAIRES** are resource-*full*. **HUMANNAIRES** are creative. We must be!

Can an air leak be plugged with wet toilet paper? With chewed bubble gum? With a piece of electrical tape? When you are living in space, it is no longer about what you need—it is about what will work. In exchange for learning to make do, **HUMANNAIRES** *become space people!*

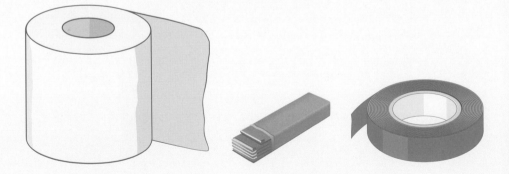

Can you eat rocks? Drink pee? Hammer in safety pins? Is algae edible? Does it taste good? Can you grow algae in space? Can aluminum foil be used for repairs? Can it be folded, frozen, broken, filed, shaped, and soldered?

Find out! Read. Experiment. Research. Repeat, and then record your findings. *Get as much experience as you can.*

You are not on your way to camp or even another country. **YOU ARE HEADED TO SPACE.** What you bring is what you have.

Every experience and type of learning you accumulate and maintain—of which *you* are certain and *you* know to be true—will make you happier, healthier, better, and safer at being who you are.

And who you are is *a person who successfully lives in space*, the very definition of a **HUMANNAIRE**.

LET'S RECAP!

At this point, **HUMANNAIRES**, we have learned:

→ **HOW HUMANKIND IS GOING TO MOVE TO SPACE...**
   IT WILL BE A SURPRISE AS THE FUTURE OF
   TECHNOLOGY AND ADVANCEMENT UNFOLDS.

→ **HOW YOU ARE GOING TO GET THERE...**
   BY PRACTICING FOCUS AND GOOD MENTAL HYGIENE.

→ **WHAT IT WILL TAKE TO LIVE IN SPACE...**
   RESOURCEFULNESS.

(A) Living in Space

One thing we do *not* know is *where* in space **HUMANNAIRES** are going to be living.

Our best answer is... *everywhere*. We may live out in space, at Lagrange points* similar to Earth, or on near-Earth asteroids, or even further out on the large asteroid Ceres.

We may live on other planets or moons in our solar system, like Mars or its moon Phobos, or Jupiter's moons Europa or Ganymede.

We may live in free-floating space colonies, or in space colonies firmly rooted on rock, or sunk into another planet's ocean.

And there are other options for space-living **HUMANNAIRES**, some of which entail drastic changes.

*Task:

*Google *Lagrange points.*

Dr. Rachel Armstrong* is a researcher studying new kinds of spacecraft. The spacecraft she imagines developing are moon-sized space colonies called *worldships.*

Dr. Armstrong imagines a new approach to building materials called "living architecture," and she believes it is possible for spaceships to be fabricated from living architecture in a way that would make them seem alive.

And there may be spaceships made of new materials that are *biomechanical*—both biological and mechanical. These worldships will use building materials that are intelligent and sensitive and even self-healing.

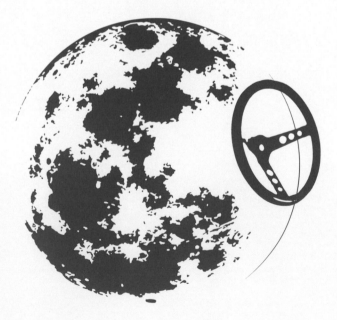

Dr. Armstrong describes worldships as natural spaceships: enormous, world-sized space carriers that are actually open to space, like a regular planet is, and generate their own heat, light,* and even other materials.

Worldships would have their own gravity. They would produce their own light.

Such a spaceship could take us anywhere because it would be like living on a planet with its own steering wheel. A worldship would be a planet that can be navigated, traveling to wherever its occupants want it to go.

We are a long way away from such worldships, but as discussed earlier, we never know what the future holds. Intelligent building materials and worldships are only a scientific breakthrough away.

*Tasks:

Google *living architect Armstrong*.
Google *bioluminescent*.

Heath Rezabek is a futurist librarian who teaches students library skills. His vision includes uploading human minds like "living books" and traveling the universe in a spaceship that is a virtual library. He calls this idea Vessel.

In Vessel, we would live virtual lives in a virtual world while our spaceship takes its time traversing solar systems and even galaxies.

The idea of Vessel is to preserve all of humankind's knowledge, like history and science and literature and DNA and records of all sorts.

However, such a visionary idea as Vessel reinvents space exploration. Living architecture and living books lead to perhaps the most challenging journey of all, and that is moving between stars across interstellar distances from our sun and our solar system to another solar system with its own sun(s)* and even another Earth.

This journey is called interstellar space exploration.

Many solar systems have more than one sun. And some solar systems have suns that are red or blue. When you look at the night sky, you can even see stars (suns) of different colors.*

*Task:

Google *binary star.*

(B) Traveling Through Space

Here are some facts about interstellar space travel and traveling between solar systems:

- ➡ **THE NEAREST SOLAR SYSTEM TO OUR OWN IS CALLED ALPHA CENTAURI B. IT IS 4.3 LIGHT YEARS AWAY FROM OUR SOLAR SYSTEM.**

- ➡ **A LIGHT YEAR IS THE DISTANCE A BEAM OF LIGHT CAN TRAVEL IN A SINGLE YEAR.**

- ➡ **THE SPEED OF LIGHT IS *186,000 MILES PER SECOND.* AT THAT SPEED, WE COULD BLINK TWICE AND BE ON THE MOON. AT THE SPEED OF LIGHT, WE COULD ARRIVE ON MARS IN ABOUT 15 MINUTES.**

- OVER INTERSTELLAR DISTANCES, THE CLOSER WE TRAVEL TO LIGHT SPEED, THE GREATER THE CHALLENGES TO BE FACED. ADVANCE TOO QUICKLY? BE MASHED BY THE RESULTANT FORCE OF ACCELERATION. INADEQUATE SHIELDING? BE COOKED BY INCREASED EXPOSURE TO RADIATION. UNINTENDED IMPACT WITH A SINGLE PIECE OF SPACE DUST? PRODUCE AN EXPLOSION POWERFUL ENOUGH TO DESTROY AN ENTIRE SPACECRAFT.

- EVEN SO, THE SPEED OF LIGHT IS THE FASTEST ANYTHING CAN GO IN OUR UNIVERSE. ALL THINGS—INCLUDING LIGHT— CAN GO ONLY AS FAST AS THE SPEED OF LIGHT, AND NO FASTER. IF THERE IS ONE TRAFFIC LAW IN THE UNIVERSE, IT IS THE SPEED LIMIT, AND THAT LIMIT IS THE SPEED OF LIGHT.

- TRAVELING FASTER THAN THE SPEED OF LIGHT IS IMPOSSIBLE. HOW IMPOSSIBLE? IT IS SO IMPOSSIBLE THAT IT IS AS IF THE UNIVERSE WERE A VIDEO GAME, AND THE SPEED OF LIGHT IS WRITTEN IN AS PART OF REALITY'S PROGRAMMING CODE.

- HOWEVER, FUTURE **HUMANNAIRE**, WHILE EVERYTHING MUST REMAIN LESS THAN THE SPEED OF LIGHT, WE HAVE SCIENTISTS TODAY WORKING ON A WAY TO MOVE *BETWEEN* THE SPEED OF LIGHT.

- INSTEAD OF GOING FASTER THAN THE SPEED OF LIGHT, WHICH IS NOT POSSIBLE, WHY NOT INSTEAD TAKE A SHORTCUT RIGHT THROUGH ORDINARY REALITY AND LET SPACE BEND AND MOVE AROUND US?

There are scientists working on this fantastic challenge at this very moment.

KIP THORNE

A professor of theoretical physics at California Institute of Technology. Professor Thorne understands that the speed of light is reality's speed limit, so what he works on is exceptional rules to ordinary physics that would allow us to travel "through" space and time and go interstellar.*

MIGUEL ALCUBIERRE

A theoretical physicist and a professor and director at the Nuclear Sciences Institute of the National Autonomous University of Mexico. Professor Alcubierre is famous for working up possible mathematics for interstellar travel. His solution is called the Alcubierre drive.*

HAROLD "SONNY" WHITE

A mechanical engineer, an applied physicist, and a propulsion scientist for NASA's Eagleworks* division. Using Professor Alcubierre's design as a model, Dr. White works on experiments to prove out the math of an Alcubierre drive.

Who knows?

Most people never believed humankind would travel to the moon. Yet we did! All it takes are breakthroughs in our understanding of energy and physics, and suddenly, one day we will find ourselves in the orbit of another earth in another solar system, getting ready to make our first contact with life from somewhere other than *our* Planet Earth.

*Tasks:

Google: *kip thorne interstellar*
alcubierre drive
nasa eagleworks

 **Aliens**

Now let's talk about aliens. Whenever anyone thinks of aliens today, we imagine all sorts of creative speculation. But the fact of the matter is that **HUMANNAIRES** may indeed be the first *monkey*-type aliens.

Without exceptional breakthroughs in technology, we will be unable to live without the atmosphere, food, fuel, and habitat we carry with us. In this way, it is exactly the same as living underwater.

Underwater in the seas, land-humans are aliens to the dolphins and whales, and to the sharks and other fishes. But the question is, aliens or not, do we belong underwater? The answer to that question is for each individual to decide for himself or herself.

Upon their first glimpse of a real shark in the water, many land-humans leave the water forever. In effect, these people *choose* to stay as land-humans.

But for some of us, meeting with our first shark is like meeting a new neighbor, with new boundaries and new rules of conduct to learn and respect.

Humans who react this way are the people who choose to be space-humans (even if only in the water). Like in the water, in space we are forever "learners."

In space, **HUMANNAIRES** become "the new neighbors," but in a neighborhood that goes on forever. And chances are when we meet our first space-shark, we will also soon encounter or learn of our first space-dolphin.

It will be in meeting our first space-dolphin that our true nature and abilities will be put to the test.

Allow me to explain.

Think of other human beings, like you, from Earth. They are the same as you. All human Homo sapiens* from Earth at this time pretty much appear the same.

There are many customs and traditions among us, some of which may be more or less agreeable to you or me, but essentially all human Homo sapiens on Earth are similar.

In fact, all of us are similar enough to communicate back and forth and to understand one another.

*Tasks:

Google _Homo sapiens_.

Now, imagine human beings from *another world.*

Imagine human people who are like you and me but are from another world
or planet with entirely different and unique experiences and customs.

You know what? Chances are in our favor that the two separate human
Homo sapien people—theirs and ours—would be able to find a common ground,
to communicate, and very possibly to get along *even with language and
cultural differences.*

Got it? Now imagine human beings from another world, human beings who look nothing like us at all.

Have you ever thought of human beings like that? Our own human Homo sapien experience has conditioned us to limit our imagination of what else is—or can be—human.

There is no rule to say that humans must look like *us* (like taller, hairless primates*). Actually, there is no rule to say that human beings must be land-humans.

This brings us to the most exciting and most challenging idea of this entire manual for you as a possible **HUMANNAIRE**. And that is this:

Is it imaginable that sea-dolphins and sea-whales are sea-humans?

*Tasks:

Yes, Google *primates.*
Google *cetacea.*
Google *"signature whistle"* in quotation marks.

Study for yourself, new **HUMANNAIRE**, and you will find that:

- ➡ SEVERAL SPECIES OF DOLPHINS AND WHALES MEET ALL INTELLIGENCE CRITERIA TO BE CONSIDERED, AT THE VERY LEAST, HUMAN THINKING.

- ➡ INTELLIGENCE AND MIND ARE NOT LIMITED BY PHYSIOLOGY OR SIZE...OR *LANGUAGE*.

- ➡ AS A MATTER OF FACT, BOTTLE-NOSED DOLPHINS, FIN WHALES, AND MANY SPECIES OF CETACEA* HAVE THEIR OWN NAMES FOR ONE ANOTHER.* NO OTHER SPECIES ON EARTH—*BESIDES HOMO SAPIENS*—HAS NAMES FOR ONE ANOTHER.

- ➡ DOLPHINS AND WHALES ARE COMMUNICATING WITH ONE ANOTHER CONSTANTLY AND ARE CAPABLE OF GREAT EMOTION.

- ➡ BUT WHAT CONFUSES US LAND-HUMANS IS THEY DO ALL THIS AND POSSIBLY DO IT USING SOMETHING BESIDES LANGUAGE AS WE UNDERSTAND IT!

(Remember, signing and signaling are forms of language. Cetacea may be communicating using a method even different than sign language.)

So the question is, how can we as Homo sapien-type humans—who use *language* in order to easily connect and share—communicate with *other* type humans who are connecting with one another by a means *other than language as we know it?*

HUMANNAIRES, whoever discovers the answer to this question may turn out to be the greatest of all **HUMANNAIRES**!

To Be Continued...

Acknowledgements

The Astronaut Instruction Manual was made possible in part because of those who preordered the book on Inkshares.com. Thank you.

Adam Gomolin	Eric Post
Alan E. Michael	Garrett O'Connell
Alma Armendariz	Gene Kiegel
Andreas C. Tziolas	Ieva Barroso
Andy Kitchar-Hatch	James M. Cooper
Antonio Estenoz III	James T. Hendrick
Bert A. Whitt	Jeannie M. McGuire
Bert Carson	Jeffrey Case
Calvin W. Allen	Joe Garcia
Chris Otten	John E. Dodds
Claude Gardner	John M. McCarter
Connie L. Fowler	John Teets
Craig Cates	Jonathan Pidgeon
Damian Vantriglia	Joseph Rozzero
Dennis Beaver	Joyce L. Hamlin
Edward Russo	Kate Miano
Elsa H. Clark	Katherine A. O'Shea
Emma Mann-Meginniss	Kendall Jones

Inkshares is a crowdfunded publisher. We democratize publishing by letting readers select the books we publish—we edit, design, print, distribute and market any book that meets a preorder threshold.

Interested in making a book idea come to life? Visit inkshares.com to find new projects or start your own.

INKSHARES

About the Author

Mike Mongo is a professional space geek. His primary objective is encouraging students worldwide to seek future careers in astronautics and space science-related fields.

Mr. Mongo is a frequent speaker on space industry councils, including the National Space Society (NSS), International Space Development Conference (ISDC), and the DARPA-funded 100 Year Starship Symposium.

Mr. Mongo is the chief brand and culture officer at Icarus Interstellar, a space research company. He lives in Key West, Florida, with his wife, Leonie, and cat, George.

TO CONTACT MIKE MONGO
VISIT HUMANNAIRE.ORG
OR EMAIL MR. MONGO AT
MM@HUMANNAIRE.ORG

Image Credits

36—"Relación entre la rueda de tipos y la impresora," Source: Biblioteca de la Facultad de Derecho y Ciencias del Trabajo.
https://www.flickr.com/photos/fdctsevilla/4074919896/

37—"Gauges," Source: Samuel Z.
https://www.flickr.com/photos/zdepth/8217551973/

61—"Rocket Garden," Source: Marcus Winter.
https://www.flickr.com/photos/ghazzog/2097082587/in/photolist-4cj6Ak-7UeXwU-aaGKgw-dUM7km-aasMh6-7F9VWc-7FdPrm-4oAGjy-dUM7bJ-4qLPy4-4tu4X3-eWGDKp-a547Rx-eWGDpv-eeb6Ng-7UbJbD-gYLv-oosBP6-pdqGCa-7iWG6Z-2EdcfS-66i6h3-3dapiB-biw5wt-6kWqv1-efuzgS-aYNQVz-o7eXgH-4Zk5GF-or6B3A-bDYC2V-56jF48-oWcHRy-ae8Ty3-FH1UW-dUZLtA-eec1PA-6SYTeK-dUFwir-aPhSr8-fTa2H-dUU9P4-dUM7g7-dUM6Zy-dUZB6w-dUZJmf-dUZHVL-dUU7WK-6zSgPA-dUU2dB

70, 71—"Page 87 of *A Whaling Cruise to Baffin's Bay and the Gulf of Boothia*," Source: The British Library.
https://www.flickr.com/photos/britishlibrary/11064018343/

71—"Charanga de Ader," Biblioteca de la Facultad de Derecho y Ciencias del Trabajo.
https://www.flickr.com/photos/fdctsevilla/4074175249/

Shutterstock Licenced Images:

xiv—"Space Shuttle," Irvan Pratama.

3—"Astronaut sign-vector symbol," murphy81.

6—"Satellite Silhouette," whitehoune.

13—"Vector illustration of human eye in vintage engraved style Isolated, grouped, transparent background," lestyan.

16—"Space Collection-vector," Tajne.

22—"Navy. A set of paths submarines. Black and white illustration of a white background," Skryl Sergey.

32—"Canada fist," NEGOVURA.

40—"Camp Camping Picnic Recreational Jungle Survivor Tool Equipment Silhouette," Leremy.

45—"Meals menu icon-hand-drawn icon set on gray circle background," ONiONA.

46—"Rock Climbing," itVega.

48—"Insulating tape," Tanya K.

48—"Chewing gum isolated-vector version," Tetiana Yurchenko.

48—"Toilet Paper," Tanya K.

49—"Science icons, doodles, chemical laboratory, a stack of books," Marina Bolsunova.

51—"Sketch of Astronaut or Spaceman Grabbing a Star," BluezAce.